Fragile Beauty

The Victorian Art of Pressed Flowers

By Sandy Puckett

Photography by Michael Chan

WARNER BOOKS

A Time Warner Company

Warner Books, Inc., 1271 Avenue of the Americas, New York, NY 10020

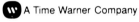 A Time Warner Company

Printed in Milan, Italy by Amilcare Pizzi S.p.A.

First printing: April 1992

10 9 8 7 6 5 4 3 2 1

Library of Congress Cataloging-in-Publication Data

Puckett, Sandy
  Fragile beauty : the Victorian art of pressed flowers / Sandy Puckett.
    p.   cm.
  ISBN 0-446-51673-2
  1. Pressed flower pictures. 2. Flowers. I. Title.
SB449.3.P7P83   1992
745.92'8—dc20   91-50410
                                                        CIP

Packaged by The Mitchell Rose Literary Agency

Photographs by Michael Chang

Cover and Interior Design by Michaelis/Carpelis Design Assoc. Inc.

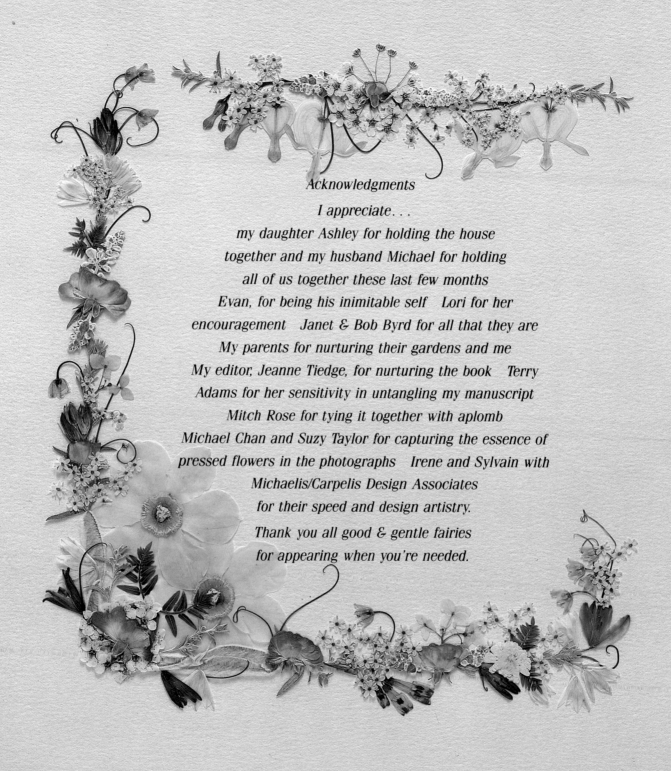

Acknowledgments

I appreciate. . .

my daughter Ashley for holding the house
together and my husband Michael for holding
all of us together these last few months
Evan, for being his inimitable self   Lori for her
encouragement   Janet & Bob Byrd for all that they are
My parents for nurturing their gardens and me
My editor, Jeanne Tiedge, for nurturing the book   Terry
Adams for her sensitivity in untangling my manuscript
Mitch Rose for tying it together with aplomb
Michael Chan and Suzy Taylor for capturing the essence of
pressed flowers in the photographs   Irene and Sylvain with
Michaelis/Carpelis Design Associates
for their speed and design artistry.

Thank you all good & gentle fairies
for appearing when you're needed.

to my Great Aunt Nan

AND TO YOU...

The art of pressed flower design, Victorian, romantic, and delicate, is a simple one. Grandmothers and aunts, gentle ladies from more gracious eras, have laced their stationery with flowers for generations, understanding and appreciating quiet pleasures: the warmth of the summer sun illuminating the colors and textures of the garden, fairies dancing on the dewdrops, the delicate scent of roses after a spring rain, the high, sweet chirp of a finch swooping homeward at twilight.

Within these pages I have conjured up this softer time, weaving flowers, fairies, and poetry into a pattern inspired by Nature, creating a book about not only pressed flower design, but about the mysterious and wonderful world of the garden and wild woods and meadows. I wish to usher you into a realm of enchantment, gilded with petals, where you may explore the

I'll give thee fairies to attend on thee;
And they shall fetch thee jewels from the deep,
And sing, while thou on pressed flowers dost sleep.

William Shakespeare, A Midsummer Night's Dream

mystical territories within yourself, and see, with crystal clarity, the wondrous universe at your feet. The illustrations—pressed flower designs—are the result of my observation of detail. I have recognized this as the source of my creative power and I encourage you to see and appreciate this hidden, precious world, to absorb it into your designs and your life.

Here, too, I hope that you will learn to see the fairies in your garden—the tiny, magical beings who bring to light the wonder of delicate growing things. Fairies instill my work with a sense of joy, making all the difference between mere craft and creative expression, between tedium and celebration. My designs are inspired when I visualize the garden fairies loosely winding silken ribbons through my pictures, gently guiding my hand, and they will do the same for you.

I offer you a light heart to enjoy the gathering of flowers and a light touch to apply those gatherings to paper with a feeling of awe and respect.

I hope that I may inspire you so that you, too, can sit in your favorite spot, morning coffee in hand, and catch the sunlight filtered through a tiny squirrel's ears, see the morning dew caught within the folds of the lady's mantle and smell the fragrance of the earth.

May my book bring you contentment with all that you have and the confidence to arrange the flowers of your world.

CONTENTS

CHAPTER ONE

TO REMINISCE

Pressing flowers is a nostalgic pastime, arousing thoughts of bygone days and genteel ways. My Great Aunt Nan, years ago, sent letters softened with a simple pressed design. Her message remains, not the ephemeral written words,

There's rosemary, that's for remembrance;
Pray you, love, remember,
And there is pansies, that's for thoughts...

William Shakespeare, Hamlet

but the love and patience that shone out, making her missives much more than long forgotten notes on a blank sheet of paper.

Remembering Aunt Nan, I recall the frost on the windows, the snow-covered yard, and her cool back room, bright with the blooming geraniums and miniature roses she kept over the winter.

Flowers, people and their gardens are woven through my earliest memories. When I was very small, my mother would set me in a big galvanized tub to play while she worked. Encircled by strawberries, carrots, poppies or peonies—whatever was in season—my tub sailed the garden sea. I can see my grandmother pinching the spent blooms from her geraniums in the mornings and my grandfather tending his gooseberries.

My own garden is a patchwork quilt, each bright square a fond memory: a trellis from a friend; the arch saved from a rubbish heap and transported two hundred miles home; fish in the pond, won at the county fair; a porch swing, a gift from my husband before we married; the millstone from a cherished country house; bird feeders hammered and painted with my children on a snowy winter day— gifts from the heart, embroidered and stitched together with flowers.

Certain flowers strike a chord, and intimate associations with flowers begin almost at birth. The pansy resembles a treasured face. Hollyhocks evoke childhood summer days when we fashioned ladies from their blooms. Pink and white carnations in dapper lapels bring back the dizzying excitement of a first dance.

3

THE FLOWERS

All the names I know from nurse:
Gardener's garters, Shepherd's purse,
Bachelor's buttons, Lady's smock,
And the Lady Hollyhock.

Fairy places, fairy things,
Fairy woods where the wild bee wings,
Tiny trees for tiny dames —
These must all be fairy names!

Tiny woods below whose boughs
Shady fairies weave a house;
Tiny tree-tops, rose or thyme,
Where the braver fairies climb!

Fair are grown-up people's trees,
But the fairest woods are these;
Where if I were not so tall,
I should live for good and all.

Robert Louis Stevenson

Like Stevenson, whose poetry has been beloved by generations of children, I have conjured up fairy images, using them to illustrate many of my ideas and to inspire my designs. Fairies have a noble geneology, alighting throughout literature in Peter Pan, Mother Goose, Grimm's and Hans Christian Andersen's fairy tales, to name a few.

The Irish, with their "little people" and shamrocks and soft secret mists, are particulalry adept at fairy detection. Thomas Crofton Croker in *Fairy Legends and Traditions of the South of Ireland* describes fairies as "a few inches high, airy and almost transparent in body; so delicate in their form that a dewdrop, when they chance to dance on it, trembles, indeed, but never breaks."

For the most part unseen, fairies ingeniously mingle with our destinies. The name itself derives from the Latin *fatum*, meaning "fate." These diminutive sprites have been known to use gardens as laboratories, casting spells with their potions of flowers and herbs.

Peer into your garden in the early evening and you will discover traces of their presence: tiny caves hidden within intricate tree roots, cobweb canopies, toadstool pavilions and snail shell castles—secret places you somehow know you are forbidden to touch.

My children and I welcome these pixies in our garden's midst, spending hours speculating on their appearance, sense of humor, lifestyle and family traditions. The world, from their miniature perspective, is an enchanting one.

Fetch me that flower; the herb I showed thee once;
The Juice of it on sleeping eyelids laid
Will make or man or woman madly dote
Upon the next live creature that it sees.

William Shakespeare, A Midsummer Night's Dream

Learning from the fairies, awakening your intimate association with flowers, you too may cast spells, luring others into a charmed world.

I imagine a universal floral subconscious, which mortals subliminally sense and dip into from time to time. The fairies act as messengers from this peaceful plane, permeating our thoughts and emerging into our feelings with disclosures of floral truths, or "jewels from the deep."

Hearing the harmonies of these truths, dwelling in spirit and substance among the green gold palette of growing things, many artists and writers immortalized their gardens in paint and prose. From the dreamily focused paintings of Monet to the rosily illustrated stories of Tasha Tudor to the gardening books of Gertrude Jekyll, stoutly Victorian, and Vita Sackville-West, gaily nonconformist in all but her formal gardens, an exhilarating array of floral bounties unfolds. There are also the enchanting flower fairies of Cicely Mary Barker, the garden animals of Beatrix Potter, and the delightful *Child's Garden of Verses* of Robert Louis Stevenson. Cherished through the years, these works are classics, beloved for their ability to pull us into their world.

With their sweet perfumes and rich blooms, flowers have traditionally marked celebrations, cascading from city gates in times of happiness and from doorways to betoken a loved one within. Wreaths and garlands, brimming with blossoms, entwined with trailing leaves and vines, even now herald special times and spe-

cial occasions. The Christmas wreath, hung on the door, welcomes the visitor and betides good cheer within, and a circle of straw, poked through with pastel bouquets, announces the arrival of spring. In Italy, the carnation was used for wreaths and garlands. The word itself derives from the Latin *corona*, meaning garland or crown, and in England, the carnation was first known as the coronation. Wild olive, dusty green and dense, crowned the victorious of the Olympic games, while Roman soldiers wore a crown of oak leaves. Laurel or bay, even parsley, garlanded Roman athletes and poets. The Greeks were the first to use flower language, or florigraphy, where different flowers represented specific emotions and ideas.

A *violet in the youth of primy nature,*
Forward, not permanent, sweet, not lasting,
The perfumes and suppliance of a minute;
No more.

William Shakespeare, Hamlet

Florigraphy enjoyed a renaissance during the romantic Victorian era when ribbons and lace, daintily printed calling cards, exquisite etiquette, and floribund expressions of sentiment were fashionable. The early Victorians added nuances by presenting the flower in different positions, such as inverting it to contradict the original meaning. Even the placement of the knot on the bouquet's ribbon was a token of hidden meaning.

Flowers have mesmerized for centuries. The rose that you hold or weave into your picture has grown from a very distinguished line. Its heritage is ancient and still it has remained true and powerfully speaks to you alone as it once did to William Shakespeare: "That which we call a rose by any other name would smell as sweet."

Working with flowers, preserving and interpreting their messages, prolonging their impact, you begin to realize that to romanticize them into beautiful designs deserves your utmost creative touch.

What follows is a list of pressing flowers and their meanings. You may discover hidden meanings of your own, as they whisper to you their secrets.

Alyssum	Worth beyond beauty
Bachelor's Button	Celibacy
Bay Leaf	I change but in death
Bay Wreath	Reward of merit
Bindweed	Passing attachment without consequence
Bluebell	Constancy and kindness
Buttercup	Cheerfulness
Chamomile	Energy in adversity. "The more it is trodden on, the faster it grows." Shakespeare
Chervil	Sincerity
Clematis	Mental Beauty
Columbine	Emblem of forsaken lovers: Purple, resolved to win; Red, anxious and trembling
Daisy	Innocence
Elderflower	Humility and kindness
Fennel	Flattery
Fern	Sincerity, fascination
Flax	Fate; I fccl your kindness

Forget-me-not	Speaks for itself
Fuschia	Amiability
Garland of flowers	Love's bondage; reward of virtue
Geranium	Folly
Goldenrod	Treasure and good fortune
Ivy	Friendship, fidelity, matrimony
Larkspur	Lightness, levity
Laurel or Bay	Glory
Lavender	Devotion; allusion to ''distrust'' based on old belief that the asp which killed Cleopatra lurked beneath lavender; approach with caution
Lily of the Valley or Lily of the May	Return of happiness
Lobelia	Malevolence
Love-in-a-Mist or Nigella	Perplexity
Lupine	Imagination
Marjoram	Blushes
Morning Glory	Affectation
Moss	Maternal love. Lapland mothers were said to wrap babies in ermine and cradle them in moss.
Myrtle	Love

Nasturtium	Patriotism
Nightshade	Silence
Pansy, Viola or Johnny Jump-Up	Love at first sight; thoughts. In Shakespeare's time, called Hearts-Ease and Love-in-Idleness
Parsley	Useful knowledge; ancient reputation as antidote for poison. Put on a plate with food served to a guest, it was a token of trust and feasting.
Phlox	Unanimity
Primrose	Early youth
Queen Anne's Lace	The Queen was making lace when she pricked her finger; thus the purple center represents a drop of her blood.
Rose	Love, beauty
Burgundy Rose	Unconscious beauty
Deep Red Rose	Bashful shame
Dog Rose	Pleasure and pain
Damask Rose	Beauty ever new
Full blown rose placed over two buds	Secrecy
Pink Rose	Our love is perfect happiness
Red and White Rose together	Unity

(Rose Continued)

Rosebud, Red	Pure and lovely
Rosebud, White	Girlhood
Rose Leaf	I am never importunate
Single Rose	Simplicity
Sweet Briar or Eglantine	Spring and poetry
Thornless Rose	Early attachment
White Rose	Silence
Yellow Rose	Jealousy
Rosemary	Remembrance
Rue	Disdain
Rye Grass	Changeable disposition
Sage	Esteem
Sheaf of Wheat	Abundance
Snowdrop	Consolation, hope
Spring Flowers which hang their heads: Daffodils, Violets, Snowdrops	Tears

Star of Bethlehem	Guidance; purity
Tendrils of climbing plants	Ties
Thyme	Activity; sweetness
Verbena	Enchantment
Verbena Wreath	Roman symbol of marriage
Veronica	Fidelity
Violet	Modesty
Yarrow	Disputes; quarrels. Common names: Soldier's Woundwort, Nosebleed, Bloodwort, Staunch Grass—to staunch flow of blood. Chemicals in plant are said to be effective in clotting blood.
Wisteria	Eastern symbol of youth and poetry

CHAPTER TWO

THE COTTAGE GARDEN AND HOW IT GREW

A harvest of peace
is produced from a seed of contentment.

Proverb

15

These trees and stones are audible to me,
These idle flowers, that tremble in the wind,
I understand their faery syllables.

Ralph Waldo Emerson

16

Gardening has a rich and varied history, from the Garden of Eden to Utopias past and present. Man has grown formal gardens, knot gardens, mazes, bedding gardens, wild gardens, rock gardens, gardens for country estates and cottage peasants. Of all gardening styles, the cottage garden appeals most to the pressed flower artist.

A cottage garden combines the formal outline and sense of enclosure of the old-fashioned garden (where flowers neatly border walks and walls) with the carefree, wild garden, where roses are bushy, climbers are rampant and tiny flowers nestle within the embrace of flowering shrubs—revealing a lush mixture of growing things, full of hidden treasures. The cottage garden continually delights and surprises as young plants become mature, and mature ones reseed themselves in unexpected places.

Our perceptions of cottage gardens have been defined by many artists and writers of the Victorian period such as Helen Allingham and Henry Stannard,

William Robinson and Gertrude Jekyll. Their interpretations often romanticized the feelings, captured in their paintings and writings, that the present cottage gardener seeks: serenity, tenderness, the soft, hushed quaintness of the Old World.

William Robinson, in *The English Flower Garden,* says, "What is the secret of the cottage garden's charms?. . . it is the absence of any pretentious "plan" which lets the flowers tell their story to the heart. The walks are only what are needed, and so we see only the earth and its blooms. . ."

The garden is an artistic and magical extention of the gardener, a mysterious reflection of the sower's joys and hopes and wishes.

You will be blending cottage charm with utility of purpose, all the endearments a garden provides with the harvest for your creations.

Begin with definition and enclosure. The background may be tall shrubs, a picket fence, or a wooden privacy fence. Against this background, where climbers roam, you may grow the tall flowers and flowering shrubs needed for a sense of wildness: delphiniums, foxgloves, lupines, mulleins, sweet annua, lilacs, butterfly bushes, hydrangeas and yuccas. Don't forget sunflowers, the giants of the daisy family, which stand sentinel over every entrance to my garden.

Arches and trellises provide vertical lines. Gracefully trailing wisteria, morning glories, trumpet vines, clematis and climbing roses add romance. The tendrils and grasping leaves of these plants and even of bindweed and wild grapevine give movement to the garden and to your designs.

Within the garden I use rocks of all interesting shapes and sizes. Granite, glinting with mica; pinkish sandstone, the color of summer sunsets or quartz, shimmering like solid moonbeams. All help tie the trees and flowers to the earth and give tiny things a place to hide. I once spent a summer hauling limestone from the nearby quarry, and now my garden is lined with the creamy white rocks, full of fossils and little depressions, where rainwater forms pools for the frogs and fairies. Majestic and beautiful stones rest in my garden, lending fluidity and texture, reminders of places I have been.

Inside these boundaries of tall plants and rocks you will plant your own vision of carefree, wild bounty. The pressed flower garden is woven into the pleasure garden, where you plant everything you like, whether it will press or not. I am never satisfied without massive plots of purple iris and pink tulips—soul flowers, not for pressing. Who can breeze through the January catalogues without yearning for wild drifts of daisies, or grape arbors and fields of strawberries? Often I plant something which I don't intend to press, and discover later the foliage is perfect for my palette. Allow yourself these unexpected encounters. If a flower or piece of foliage is not there, in your garden, its pressing possibilities may escape you.

Years ago I encircled the front of our little house in the country with Heavenly Blue Morning Glories. Gleefully, they cascaded across the electric wires and en-

When but a half-hour's roam through such a place
Would leave behind a dance of images,
That shall break in upon his sleep for weeks.

William Wordsworth

twined the catalpa tree twelve feet away in vibrant blooms. Hummingbirds, framed in lush blue and green, visited right up to the picture window. The morning glories didn't press well, but the tendrils and new leaves, perfectly folded hearts, were, and are, precious in my designs.

The trumpet vine, with its large showy flowers, has tiny new foliage, good for pressing, and the young foliage of wisteria adds poetry to my pictures. You may wonder that anything gets an opportunity to mature in a presser's garden, because so many of the babies are "pinched," but everything grows and flourishes. Even the prunings are used.

Tubs and pots of annuals such as lobelia provide pressing materials and fill in blank spaces in the garden as the need arises. Fuschias, those gaudy flowers loved by Victorians, are lovely when pressed. Pots of geraniums are utilitarian. The buds remain dark red when pressed, useful in holiday pictures of red and green.

The pressing garden holds the flowers that will make your pictures; so try to plant with an eye toward what you will want and need in the coming months. If you dislike orange, don't plant it. Sow colors that appeal to you; this will give cohesion to your garden and your designs as well.

You will need flowers in a variety of colors and textures, but keep in mind that the garden should not be fussy and patchy. The eye should be rested, not bounced here and there. Create a harmony of color and a feeling of tranquility. Your garden is a living picture, an immersion into color and scent, and all the flowers, shrubs and vines are gently flowing parts of the whole. One way to view your garden for the overall plan is to survey it from above, an upstairs window or balcony. Another viewpoint is from a lawn chair, as a visitor quietly absorbing the ambiance.

You may unify your plantings with drifts of buttercups, daisies, loosestrife, Fairy roses, the artemisias, and lamb's ears. These drifts are the watercolor wash for your gardening palette. Allowing the tides of color to ebb and flow, you may end up with an abundance of one or two varieties of flowers. I have a wealth of larkspur and calendulas, while a friend has a surfeit of wild phlox and perennial geraniums. We trade, expanding our gardens and our time together. The more gardening friends you have, the more beautiful and varied your garden and theirs will be. Thus the term "friendship garden"—what every garden can ultimately become.

Tuck your little plants in and gather the whole together. Many good perennials take two or three years to come into their own. Until they mature, fill the space they will require with annuals needed for pressing.

A pressed flower garden provides tiny jewels and inspirations, smaller pictures within the larger canvas of your garden. Each little vignette has its own appeal, its own family of fairies, enchanting in their own way: a patch of forget-me-nots magically reseeding beneath the Fairy roses, or pert pansies peeking up between

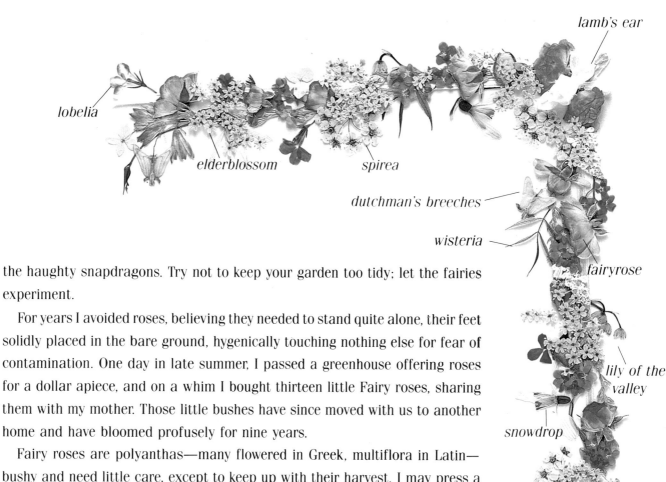

lamb's ear

lobelia

elderblossom

spirea

dutchman's breeches

wisteria

fairyrose

lily of the valley

snowdrop

wood hyacinth

snowball

morning glory vine

the haughty snapdragons. Try not to keep your garden too tidy; let the fairies experiment.

For years I avoided roses, believing they needed to stand quite alone, their feet solidly placed in the bare ground, hygenically touching nothing else for fear of contamination. One day in late summer, I passed a greenhouse offering roses for a dollar apiece, and on a whim I bought thirteen little Fairy roses, sharing them with my mother. Those little bushes have since moved with us to another home and have bloomed profusely for nine years.

Fairy roses are polyanthas—many flowered in Greek, multiflora in Latin—bushy and need little care, except to keep up with their harvest. I may press a book of them every day in the early summer and again from late summer into fall. The house always has a blue bowl of pink Fairy roses, and still I have more than enough to share.

Every year I grow more roses, realizing what the poets were rambling about. A constant source of color from June until after the first frost, they form the inspiration for many pressed designs and a lovely focal point in the garden.

The following pages illustrate the pressing flowers.

From the initiation of the Fairy roses, I have moved on to any rambling, free flowing or cluster rose. Their drama is essential for pressed flowers. Recently I have rediscovered my Aunt Nan's miniature roses, wonderful in the garden for not only color but their extra fine foliage. They may be moved into the house in winter to pick, press and enjoy during the cold months.

What a splendid exercise it would be if people would only go round their places and look for all the ugly corners and just think how they might be made beautiful by the use of free-growing Roses.

Gertrude Jekyll, Roses

22

*T*here's fennel for you, and columbines.
There's rue for you, and here's some for me;
We may call it herb of grace o'Sundays.
You must wear your rue with a difference.
There's daisy. I would give you some violets,
But they withered all when my father died.

William Shakespeare, Hamlet

24

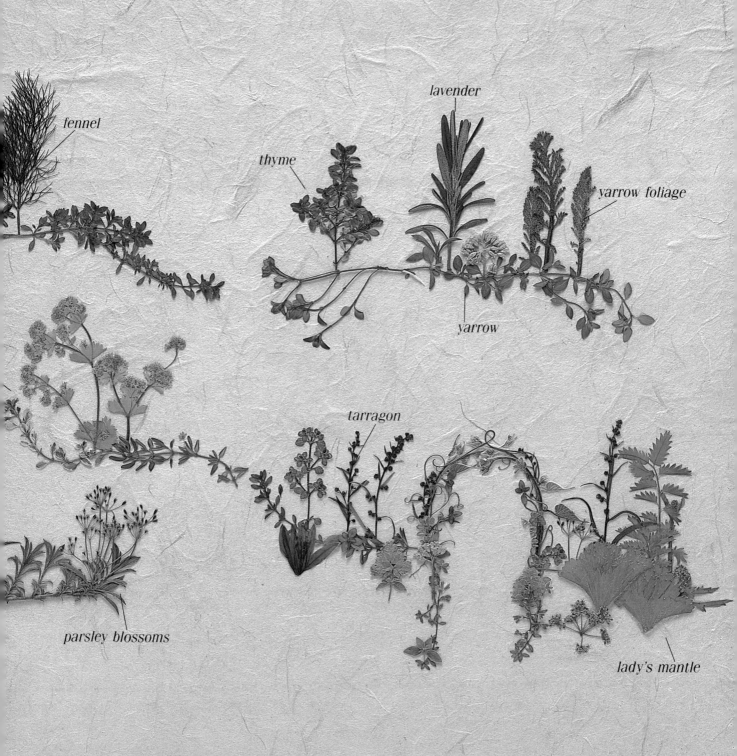

fennel

thyme

lavender

yarrow foliage

yarrow

tarragon

parsley blossoms

lady's mantle

daisy

nasturtium

pansy

nasturtium bud

columbine

lobelia

crocus

buttercup

verbena

wood hyacinth

nightshade

*The foolish man seeks happiness in the distance,
the wise grows it under his feet.*

James Oppenheimer

viola

impatiens bud

larkspur

primrose

perennial geraniums

salvia

queen anne's lace

bluebell

larkspur

lobelia

scilla

baby's breath

bluebell

salvia

lav

alyssum

lobelia

lily of the valley

forget-me-nots

salvia

fairyrose

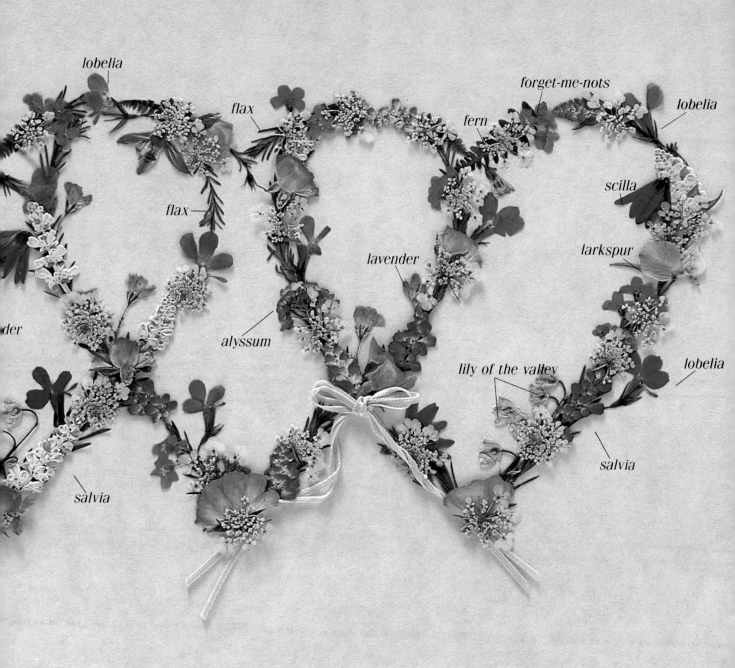

*The cost of a thing is the amount of what I will call life which is required
to be exchanged for it.*

Henry David Thoreau

The wealth of your garden is not how much you have but how much you enjoy.
Take pleasure in it and your labor there will be both satisfying and rejuvenating.
If it is not, you may be trying to control too much. I have seen many slaves to
their gardens, exchanging too much life, always working, never dreaming or realizing
the presence of the fairies in the flowers. I force nothing in my garden, including
myself. Occasionally the garden nudges me with its needs and I respond.

An observant and resourceful person needs no garden other than the woods
and meadows, the roadside verges in spring, or the vacant fields and sidewalk
cracks of the city. A friend, artist and lifetime presser I admire has one pot of
flowers on her terrace.

The garden, whatever its size, is a tranquil avenue leading to self-expression.
Our children have grown with the garden; every niche has been nursery, gover-
ness and playmate.*

31

* From the time they could walk, our son Evan and daughter Ashley have been playing
  with unseen companions in the tree roots and rocks.

When children are playing alone on the green,
In comes the playmate that never was seen.

Robert Louis Stevenson, The Unseen Playmate

We have consciously woven fairy legends into our children's lives. These dreaming times allow us to share our thoughts with our children and give them a framework within which to share with us.

Ashley once left this message on my answering machine, a product of our musings together: "Mrs. Puckett: This is Cecily from the Trading Company. I'm calling to inform you that your Garden Fairies have arrived. I believe it is the Huckleberry Family. There's Father Eldon, Mother Rose, a little girl, Poppy, and her tiny brother, Bowen. Bowen has a slightly damaged wing. All seems to be in good order, but I would appreciate it if you would pick them up at your earliest convenience as they are anxious to be free and out of their little traveling basket. They've come a long way and they're tired."

The fishpond has been christened Iris Lake and last summer hosted an elaborate rabbit wedding.

My garden has been a pirate ship, Barbie Doll vacation paradise, Sylvanian Family campground, jungle, maze, obstacle course, arena for birthday treasure hunts, and the Yukon for Calvin and Hobbes. It is well peopled.

To the fairy land afar
Where the Little People are;
Where the clover-tops are trees,
And the rain-pools are the seas,
And the leaves like little ships
Sail about on tiny trips. . .

Robert Louis Stevenson, The Little Land

In the summer we break ''Fairy Bread'' in the garden for tea, celebrating both the moment and the ritual. Easter, for us, is a celebration of spring when we hide tiny baskets with small, precious things, gifts from the fairies within. During the Holidays, we front a printer's drawer with our own Advent calendar. Each little door opens to a miniature gift, suitable only for small people. On Christmas morning, we wake to a tiny tree with miniature gifts. The fairies are always with us, making homework difficult, for they beckon the children outdoors to play.

Children, friends and family all contribute to the garden and the garden to them. The greatest achievement of your garden will be the sense of timelessness it creates. Peace and wonder will flow into your life.

34

But the lesson I have thoroughly learnt, and wish to pass on to others, is to know the enduring happiness that the love of a garden gives. . .For love of gardening is a seed that once sown never dies, but always grows and grows to an enduring and ever-increasing source of happiness. . . Each new step becomes a little surer, and each new grasp a little firmer, till, little by little, comes the power of intelligent combination, the nearest thing we know to the mighty force of creation.

Gertrude Jekyll

CHAPTER THREE

GATHERING AND PRESSING

Gathering your flowers is an intimate adventure, for now the tiny details of the garden let themselves be known. You see your flowers from a new perspective, that of the fairies. Common weeds are suddenly magical things. After the morning dew has lifted, go into the garden with a medium-sized basket, and

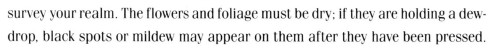

To see a world in a grain of sand
And a heaven in a wild flower,
Hold Infinity in the palm of your hand
And Eternity in an hour.

William Blake

36

survey your realm. The flowers and foliage must be dry; if they are holding a dewdrop, black spots or mildew may appear on them after they have been pressed.

Begin your pressing path with the least fragile plants, those which will survive longest in the bottom of your basket. On hot summer days, when the temperature soars above ninety degrees and blossoms wilt quickly, be careful to gather for no more than five or ten minutes at a time, pressing each batch immediately. Gently pinch off anything which speaks to you, looking at everything with the eye of the artist—tiny tendrils of morning glories wrapped around the lilac bush; very young, blue salvia spikes, mimicking buds of lavender; foliage of interest and texture. You will need at least as much foliage as flowers, for it is the basis of your designs. Pick anything that fills you with wonder.

The flowers you will not use are those with an extremely high water content and the large flowers like zinnias or marigolds, which are happiest in bouquets.

You will be amazed at the scope of your pressing garden. Wheat, ornamental and wild grasses are especially delicate. Be sure to press the tiniest things. In the abundance of the outdoors, when you are picking, a single stem of rye grass may look insignificant, but once it is on a piece of pink parchment, it may very well define your entire design.

Gather a variety of flowers, herbs, and grasses in every season. Some things bloom all summer; others must be harvested at specific times to look their best when pressed. Silver King artemisia is at its best for only about two weeks, immediately before it blooms. Sweet annua, gathered in autumn, has a golden tinge, and Dutchman's breeches offers its delicate blossoms in spring.

When your basket is almost full, bring it into the house. The fruits of your labor will reflect the season, purples and golds in the fall, pinks and pastels in spring, overflowing with color in summer.

Turn the flowers out onto a piece of newspaper at a table where you may sit comfortably for an hour or so. Open a large metropolitan phone book. Its thirsty pages will drink up the moisture of the flowers, unlike glossy magazines or catalogues. Begin at the back and lay each flower and piece of foliage carefully on the page, exactly as you want it to appear when pressed. Some flowers are easy to press; the tips of the salvia spike lay any way, pressing perfectly. The graceful stems of lobelia should remain attached to the flower. Yarrow, with its tiny clusters of flowers, must be placed head-down with the stem facing you, in order to keep the full effect when pressed. Queen Anne's lace may be pressed in one large piece, but each verbena flower of the cluster must be pressed separately.

Don't force anything. The gentle curves of the leaves and foliage will add grace to your pictures. Thyme grows creeping along the ground and achieves wonderful shapes for which you will be thankful when beginning your designs. Morning glory vines should be left to curl and loop as they will.

I put a variety of color combinations on each page. Opening the book, after six weeks, each page is almost a complete palette of colors, inspirational in itself. Otherwise, you would have to go through several books to find the assortment of flowers needed to complete one picture. My books are organized according to what was growing the day I pressed rather than in books of colors or species.

Remember to put flowers of the same thickness on the same page. In this way no flower will have any breathing room, ensuring the most paper/petal contact possible. A rosebud should not be placed alongside paper thin lobelia, or the tinier blossom may curl up its edges in the gap left by its chubbier companion. Thick rosebuds may be sliced in half vertically with a sharp knife.

When each page is full, with no flowers touching, gently turn a one-quarter inch thickness of pages forward, not disturbing the flowers so carefully set. Continue this process until the book is full and gently bulging. In an hour you may fill one to three phone books, depending on the size of the flowers and the size of the books. Label the bindings with the date and names of the flowers within. If you are beginning, you may want to note the weather conditions of the day. Should your flowers not press to your liking, you will have a variable that can be changed.

Stack the phone books in an out of the way but accessible place and put an enormous amount of weight on them. I place three or four heavy patio blocks on each stack, with a board over the top book to evenly distribute the weight. This is about sixty pounds of pressure so handle carefully!

During the high summer days of pressing, you may have five stacks of two books each at any time. You may want to check on a page of particularly delicate blooms after a few days, and transfer them to a dry page. Spirea and Queen Anne's lace

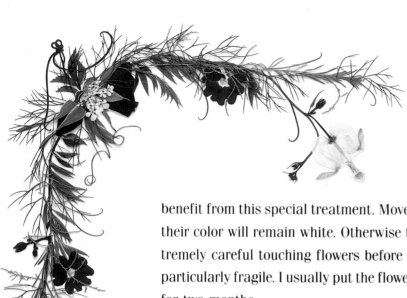

benefit from this special treatment. Move them to a dry page now and then and their color will remain white. Otherwise they may emerge a pale cream. Be extremely careful touching flowers before they are dry, for at this time they are particularly fragile. I usually put the flowers in their books and forget about them for two months.

You will know your flowers are pressed and ready for designing when they are paper thin, dry, and delicate to the touch.

Press the same variety of flower on many different days. You would not want to press all the alyssum needed for a year at once. That would be putting all your flowers in one basket, so to speak! If the weather was unfavorable, you might end up with nothing. If you press often, your rate of success will be higher. During the course of the seasons, the color of the same flower changes. Fairy roses, delicate pink in the heat of summer, become brilliant, almost hot pink when cool weather arrives, making a last bold statement before they sleep.

Many potential artists, having pressed only once and obtained poor results, have never tried again. Yet any number of things could have gone wrong that first time: the day was wet, the flowers were unsuitable for pressing, there was not enough weight on the books, the paper was not absorbent. Don't be discouraged. One entire book may be lost, but another may hold pages of inspiration.

When a book has been pressed for six weeks to two months, it is finished and ready for use. You may remove the weights and store the books anywhere that's convenient. Try to keep the temperature and humidity constant wherever the flowers are resting. Basements, often damp, and attics, where hot air rises and lingers, are unsuitable, but workrooms, cupboards, or closets, even the secret spaces under the bed, make perfectly acceptable storage spots.

Remember that it's important to gather and press throughout the year: spring bulbs, summer's flowers and foliage, autumn weeds, and winter's indoor blooms all have their own distinct personalities.

You may want to keep a traveling press—a phone book and patio block—in your car so the jewels you find in the fields and woods don't wither before you get them home.

Children make wonderful scouts for new pressing material. It seems no matter how well we have trained our adult eyes the little ones see the most lovely blooms. I have enlisted my children's small pressing fingers, at first for the simple things, artemisias and bleeding hearts, and as their coordination develops, annual verbenas and tendrils. In this way, through pressing, they have painlessly become acquainted with the flowers and the seasons.

When pressing becomes tedious, they stop, never forgetting what the flowers look like and how they smell. The same is true for you. If you only picked and pressed and never made a single design, you would be richer for it.

CHAPTER FOUR

*T*HE ART OF DESIGN

*T*he secret of designing with pressed flowers is in envisioning your goal and working toward that effect. Allow yourself to dream of beautiful things. I sometimes imagine the little bluebirds in Disney's wonderful animation, singing while they drape Cinderella in her gown for the ball, or the first gentle snow of winter lacing the garden, and I capture those images with the tools at my fingertips, the flowers and foliage I have gathered and preserved through the year.

Thoreau wrote, "Associate reverently, as much as you can, with your loftiest thoughts." You cannot fail. Your designs will be exquisite because of the person you express through them: yourself.

*P*erhaps the reward of the spirit who tries
is not the goal but the exercise.

E.V. Cooke

In art the hand can never execute anything higher than the heart can inspire.

Ralph Waldo Emerson

And 'tis my faith that every flower
Enjoys the air it beathes.

William Wordsworth

Each design should make its own statement. Don't crowd too much into it or it will become cluttered and lose its focus. Let the flowers breathe. Choose one thing to say in each piece: pastel delicacy, a blue mood, dramatic movement.

Allow the flowers (and fairies) to sing their song and speak for themselves. Be receptive to the messages they bring.

Study the intricacy of every leaf and petal, the myriad delicate details before you: the veins of the exquisite bleeding heart, the perfection and freshness of the tiny forget-me-not, the gentle shape of wheat. You will find enchantment and inspiration in the flowers. Enhance their inherent beauty in your designs. Don't force them to be something they are not or coerce them to associate with others that do not bring out their best qualities. Encourage, instead, complementary associations of color, texture, size, shape, and line.

Some flowers and colors will stir you more than others, and you will discover your own particular jewels as you work among the bounteous treasure from your cache.

Trust these vibrations within yourself. Work with the flowers that move you so that you, in turn, can move others.

There are four basic elements of pressed flower design: color, shape, line, and proportion. Every design should have an overall sense of color, a basic shape, good lines, and should use flowers of the same proportion. Sometimes one or two of the elements is stressed more than others. When you begin each design,

44

In every man's heart there is a secret nerve that answers to the vibrations of beauty.

Christopher Morley

try to think in these terms and decide which element will be most important for that particular design.

Wherever you find your inspiration, be it color, shape, line, or proportion, it is important not to neglect the other elements. Always take care that your colors are complementary, your flowers are in proportion, your lines have grace of movement, and the overall shape is pleasing and balanced.

Designing with pressed flowers is both stimulating and challenging. Orchestrating colors, textures and proportions requires, as Gertrude Jekyll said, "the power of intelligent combination."

The possibilities of these combinations are endless. You may rearrange time and nature, pairing white bleeding hearts, blooming in the spring, with creamy elderblossoms, blooming in the summer, or autumn goldenrod with winter's indoor geraniums.

Now is the time to collect your flowers and your memories, along with an assortment of pretty papers and ribbons. Gather them all together and experiment with color combinations and moods.

I know of nothing less expensive than ribbons which can bring as much enjoyment and sense of wealth. A basket of ribbons, kept nearby, is useful in so many ways. They mark special places in books, tie bundles of letters, drape through a wreath or tie bunches of lavender or wheat. Everyday enjoyment of satin and velvet ribbons adds a soft touch to the most everyday things. Tiny ribbons with pressed flowers add texture and carry out a color theme to completion.

Papers are the foundation for your designs. Pastel parchment paper, delicate rice paper, cream linen paper, crisp white handmade paper, thick textured French watercolor paper, all promote a mood with their subtle colors and textures.

A pink satin ribbon entwined in a wreath with pressed pink fairy roses and tiny blue forget-me-nots, placed on a sheet of pink parchment, speaks of delicacy and gentleness. Bold purple pansies, blue satin paper, and dark green morning glory tendrils wound around a soft blue ribbon bring to mind the freshness of the garden after a spring rain. Cream linen paper, cream satin ribbon, dark red roses, and Queen Anne's lace conjure up snowy winter nights, candlelight, and beautiful women in deep red velvet, lace and pearls.

This power of combination and sensual association is at your fingertips. The papers, ribbons, and flowers will excite and inspire you, leading you into new realms of creativity.

Often I begin thinking of a design in terms of color, visualizing a tiny pink wreath or a spray of blue across the top of a sheet of creamy stationery.

Sometimes a design begins with a specific shape. Imagine not only creating heart shapes but hearts entwined with flowers, each flower representing specific emotions: the binding tendrils of ivy, with lily of the valley gently curving toward the top of the heart, representing return of happiness. Visualize not only wreaths but little fairy rings woven with flowers of delicate pink roses and blue salvia tips, sprinkled with elderblossoms. Imagine a garland as an arch of celebration, of love, happiness and spring. Weave it of dark green flax foliage with white and crimson roses.

Other times I begin visualizing a design in terms of line. A stalk of wheat, bent by the summer breeze, or a sweet pea tendril, gaily twining about itself, may spark my imagination. The designs with line as their focus resemble watercolor paintings, the tendrils and foliage creating graceful movement.

Finally, proportion may be the source of inspiration for a design. Leafing through my archives, I may happen upon one perfectly shaped, large red rose. The design may be structured around that one perfect blossom with all the other flowers and foliage matching it in proportion: larger deep green rose foliage and deep red verbena flowers—also quite large—for accent.

The following pages illustrate designs inspired by the various elements. Each and every design, in order to be pleasing, must, of course, incorporate all the elements. These are my special combinations—the colors, shapes, lines, proportions, and flowers that release the most resonant and harmonious vibrations for me. Perhaps some of them will strike a chord in you, too.

Designs stressing color often begin with paper and ribbon. Weaving a ribbon through a wreath carries out a color theme beautifully.

*E*very artist dips his brush in his own
soul, and paints his own nature
into his pictures.

Henry Ward Beecher

49

This design is fashioned of dramatic red roses and green foliage which contrast sharply with the cream paper, ribbon and lace. (The lace must be attached first, gently dabbed with glue. Then add the ribbon.) A romantic Victorian valentine is created by working on heavy stationery and folding it in half.

50

Garden scenes are a challenging
test of proportion. Familiar flowers and
foliage take on a completely
different dimension when seen from a
fairy-sized perspective.

Large bold pansies create a
design that must include flowers of similar
proportion.

 *rifles make perfection, and perfection is no trifle.*

Michelangelo

Letters of the alphabet, penciled first on paper, require flowers of the same small proportion. One large pansy would be out of place here!

53

Line is one of my favorite starting points for design. I love the lines of barren winter trees against the sky, the lines of a cat, the lines of a face. Lines in pressed flower design carry out or create graceful movement. No foliage expresses this as well as small wisteria leaves.

*E*verything should be made
as simple as possible, but not simpler.

Albert Einstein

54

The lines of wild wheat in this simple design make a delicate statement.

Many times you will begin your pressed flower designs with a preconceived shape: wreaths, garlands, hearts, and ornate Victorian ovals. The overall size you desire for your pictures and the shape you sketch will naturally determine the size of your flowers. Remember to mix your palette carefully.

56

Beauty is not caused. It is.

Emily Dickinson

Part of the joy of pressed flower designing is sharing your enthusiasm with others. Children are very receptive to this art form. I have most enjoyed myself teaching very young children in the classroom the simple pleasures of making bookmarks. Within twenty minutes they are mentally soaring into their mother's gardens, gathering more and more flowers to create treasures to give to others. One little boy I taught said, holding up his bookmark, ''This looks like a painting!''

Another way to introduce children to pressed flowers is through thumbprint art. This provides very young children with a focus for their first designs and encourages their imaginations.

They may fold a piece of paper in half and dip their thumb into an inkpad or a dab of watercolor paint and transfer this onto the paper. With a pen they can draw a little tail and whiskers, or make the same from grass and tendrils. A money plant becomes a balloon soaring in the air. You will notice that children begin looking at flower petals more closely, discovering their intricacy, wondering if they can be used in their pictures.

These unique children's invitations and stationery, can be personalized by the little sender.

Happiness is not a destination. It is a method of life.

Burton Hills

Flower presses are found in children's stores and are easier for them to handle than patio blocks and phone books. Children need to check their flowers often, sometimes two or three times a day, and the small flower presses encourage their curiosity while saving Mother a lot of lifting.

As you design, you will begin to see a cycle develop: of planning, planting, harvesting, creating and sharing, using your carefully preserved flowers in the winter and beginning to press again in the spring. You will find yourself thinking of your flowers in terms of color and texture, shape, line and proportion, viewing your garden not only for the beauty it radiates before you but as the bountiful source for your inspired designs.

CHAPTER FIVE
GIVING PLEASURES

Pressed flowers are part of the natural world, and, like everything organic, they change. This fragility is their beauty. What you have created today will survive far longer than a dozen roses, but not as long as an oil painting. The flowers will fade, gracefully, over the course of many years, becoming more treasured and cherished as time goes by. There are antique pressed flowers that are still beautiful, though pale.

Some precautions should be taken to extend the life of your work. Avoid exposing your designs to direct sunlight, fluorescent lighting, or damp places. Your flowers, like your dreams, are delicate. Treat them gently, and enjoy them while you can.

We tire of those pleasures we take, but never of those we give.

John Petit-Senn

When you give a pressed flower design, which you have created from your garden, the moment of giving will live longer than the design itself. The joy and delight reflected back to you when someone receives your keepsake is touching and lasting.

Bookmarks, for example, will live on for years, a constant reminder of the garden and simple pleasures. I have described how to make a finished bookmark in the Appendix, but I cannot describe how very lovely they are. Almost translucent, they may be held up to the light so that you may trace every vein of every flower. They are still, to me, one of the greatest joys stemming from pressed flower work. The many colors of rice papers and ribbons make them endlessly appealing— red and green flowers on crisp white rice paper for Christmas gifts, pastels for Easter presents, deeper tones for autumn celebrations. Inserted into a children's book they add a special touch. Who cannot find a place for another bookmark? Tucked into a greeting card, a gardening book or a volume of Shakespeare, they become a secret surprise. They are such small gifts yet the joyous response they evoke cannot be measured.

Stationery and notecards are also wonderful avenues for pressed flowers. A plain notecard with a simple design will travel in the mail unprotected except for its envelope. Glue the design, a tiny spray of bleeding hearts or a shower of forget-me-nots, directly onto the notecard, adding a satin bow or satin ribbon line across the bottom or side, if you wish to carry out the color theme. Some-

61

*That man is the richest
whose pleasures are the cheapest.*

Henry David Thoreau

times I cover the notecard with a loose piece of glycerine or tracing paper, cut to size. This not only further protects the flowers but when the receiver opens the envelope, the tracing paper gives the flowers an initial softened effect.

Notecards make wonderful Old World invitations. Why not invite a few special friends for tea, using your own little design? The invitation will make a lasting remembrance.

Gift bags are transformed with pressed flowers. Use plain white bags and glue a small design directly at the top of one side. Carry out the color theme of the flowers with matching tissue. You might even punch a hole in a pressed flower notecard and tie it with a satin ribbon to the handle. A little bag of your own creation, filled with bunches of lavender and potpourri, makes a delightful hostess present.

Gifts from the heart are memorable ways to use and enjoy your pressed flowers. Often I am asked "What do I do with my pressed flowers?" The answer is simple. Give them away with gladness.

Once you have perfected the art of designing your pressed flowers, you may want to preserve them within a frame. I have described in the Appendix how to make a framed piece. The same principles apply to any size design, using any flowers. You may first want to make a standard size piece to fit a ready-made frame: $5'' \times 7''$, $8'' \times 10''$ or $11'' \times 14.''$ As you develop your style, you may find a certain size is more appealing to you. I prefer very small framed pieces. A $5'' \times 5''$ is precious, perfectly fitting for a tiny wreath. (See page 43.)

The $6'' \times 11''$ size is good for a small spray or double heart. (See page 45.) They make wonderful wedding gifts, especially the entwined hearts with the names of the bride and groom and the wedding date lightly inscribed on the matboard.

A more ambitious piece using a 16″ × 16″ frame gives the artist much more freedom. Columbines, pansies, larger roses, even poinsettia leaves may then be used. These may become quite expensive to frame and mat. You may wish to reserve them for special gifts, a parents' wedding anniversary, your daughter's graduation, or husband's birthday. Often larger pictures look more striking double matted to subtly bring out the colors of the flowers within. Remember not to get too creative with the matting and framing. The flowers are the focus.

I prefer to work most of my designs on cream matboard. Cream is a warm, neutral color which accents any flowers I choose to use. The outer, framing, mat is generally the same color if my design is small.

I always have my mats and frames professionally cut with a 1/4″ foamcore spacer between the outer mat and the mat the flowers are glued on. This spacer allows the flowers to breathe and lends it a subtle shadow box effect. If a flower should happen to dislodge itself from the design, it can fall within the space provided and not be a distraction.

Allow yourself the time and effort to dignify your work with a good mat and frame. I have so often seen beautiful pressed flower pieces placed, unmatted, in a poorly made frame. What you have created is the culmination of months of gardening and pressing. It is a statement of achievement and deserves to be respected and honored. If it is worth framing, it is worth framing well.

Framed wedding invitations are romantic reminders of a special day. I often use flowers with special significance—lavender for devotion, ivy for fidelity, or flowers such as bleeding hearts, lily-of-the-valley and roses.

As you develop your skills, you will want to try all sizes of framed pieces. Long thin 7″ × 36″ sprays are beautiful over the tops of doorways. A framed collection of herbs is wonderful in the kitchen.

My favorite use for pressed flowers is the tea tray. I love pretty things which are also functional, making everyday activities special.

We often miss breakfast or lunch at our house, but we all try to be home in time for tea. It's the quiet time of the day when we stop to talk to one another, not about homework and bills but about the pleasantries and joys of our lives. We dream, we plan new rooms for the miniature dollhouses, we discuss the delicacies we will make for tea tomorrow, we admire the pretty plates we've found at the flea market, holding our tiny sandwiches. We talk to our dog and give her delectables. Our worries are forgotten and a cozy togetherness and peace is shared.

Many trays can be purchased with a glass top and a removable bottom, especially at antique stores. Simply detach the bottom and replace it with a matboard cut to size with your pressed flower design. There may not be room for either a spacer or a mat. That's fine, although you may wish to work a ribbon through your design for added interest or use an outside border of lace, taking care to choose colors that are soft and serene, and match your teapot and cups. Be sure to glue a piece of felt to the underside so the tray doesn't scratch your table.

*There are few hours in life
more agreeable than the hour dedicated
to the ceremony known as
afternoon tea.*
Henry James, The Portrait of a Lady

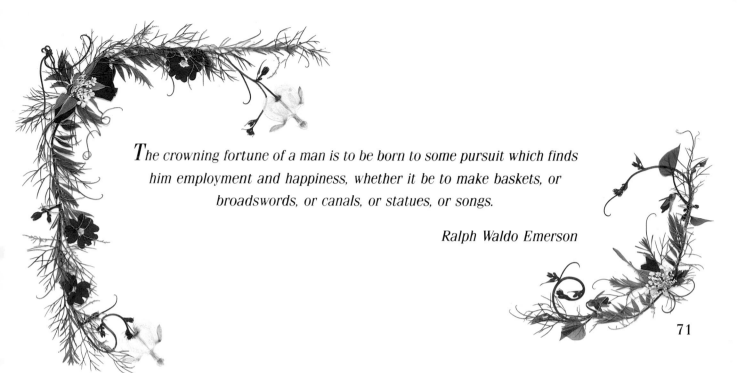

The crowning fortune of a man is to be born to some pursuit which finds him employment and happiness, whether it be to make baskets, or broadswords, or canals, or statues, or songs.

Ralph Waldo Emerson

Tea trays make wonderful gifts when you add a lace cloth and napkins, a teapot, or your favorite recipe for tea time treats.

These pleasures, these gifts, will not only nourish you as you are creating them, but also those to whom they will be given. Your children, your family, and your friends will remember the flowers and the garden and all things green and growing, even in the dark afternoons of winter.

When I finish a design it gives me something in return, intangible but nevertheless real. Sometimes the gift is almost in the form of music, distant flutes, or violins or cellos, fairy music of tinkling bells. Within a well-executed design, fairies seem to dance, bringing to life the flowers, the foliage, and the composition as a whole. Hear the music and share in the dance.

CHAPTER SIX

CELEBRATIONS

Hand in hand with fairy grace
Will we sing, and bless this place...

William Shakespeare, A Midsummer Night's Dream

Flowers celebrate life. We give flowers for all the celebrations of our lives: new babies, weddings, anniversaries, Mother's Day, Easter, birthdays. Even the solemn moments of passing are commemorated with the gift of life, flowers. Working with pressed flowers, you see these floral offerings from a whole new perspective, hearing their special truths, magically understanding the messages of Nature.

73

Working with pressed flowers is a cycle that brings you full circle. Gardening—planting and nurturing your flowers—extends you physically and socially. Gathering the flowers trains your eyes to look and see within and without. Pressing gives you the insight to foretell the juxtaposition of flowers you will be working with months in the future. Designing with the flowers you have pressed satisfies you aesthetically. The completed picture gives you enthusiasm to go back to the garden and cultivate again.

To create with pressed flowers, you must be a gardener, at least in spirit, because a gardener above all else is a dreamer. And you must be an artist, endeavoring to express your dreams.

Pressing flowers is a gentle, leisurely art form, equally suited to the young and the old, the millionaire and the pauper, rewarding every aspirant with riches beyond measure.

All of Nature contributes to your art: caterpillars and tadpoles, squirrels and bunnies, blue jays, cardinals, and humming birds, thunder and lightning, sun and rain, snow and wind and fog, creating a palette of familiar colors and textures.

Gently, I encourage you to celebrate this planet on which we tread, to take time, let the grass grow a little higher, let the weeds come on a little more while you sit and watch the fairies tickle the cat's ears. Hold your children a little tighter. Press these times into your heart. It is from these quiet, still moments that you will draw your energy.

Through these pages we have woven our way, through gardens and fairy sanctuaries. We have explored the possibilities of pressed flower designs and we have shared with others.

My hope now is that you have become inspired not only to garden enthusiastically and with an added focus but also to take pleasure in the small threads that make up the pattern of your life.

I only wish I could be there when you have made your first design and say, "Look what I've made!" The flowers will be looking back at you, whispering, "Look what we have done."

Congratulations all.

From Nature doth emotion come, and moods
Of calm equally are Nature's gift:
This is her glory; these two attributes
Are sister horns that constitute her strength
Hence Genius, born to thrive by interchange
Of peace and excitation, finds in her
His best and purest friend; from her receives
That energy by which he seeks the truth
From her that happy stillness of mind
Which fits him to receive it when unsought.

William Wordsworth, The Prelude

75

$\mathcal{A}$PPENDIX

CREATING A BOOKMARK

Materials You Will Need:

Tweezers	*Tiny ribbon*	*Hole punch*
Rice paper (found in	*Small flowers and*	*Pencil*
artist supply store)	*Foliage*	*Storebought bookmark*
Clear Contac paper	*Scissors*	*White glue*

1. Lay a standard bookmark onto your rice paper and trace its shape with a pencil. Let's use a pale pink sheet of rice paper as an example. Cut the rice paper a little larger than the pencil trim line.

2. Remember to handle your flowers and foliage only with the tweezers. They are very fragile and can break easily.

3. Pull the flowers needed for the bookmark from your phone book archives. The bookmark is small and delicate, so similar foliage will work best. Now is the time to decide on a palette of colors, plan proportions and lines. With the pink rice paper, we might choose Silver King artemisia, small blue buds of Victoria salvia, deep blue Crystal Palace lobelia, a pale pink fairy rose and some delicate white Queen Anne's lace.

4. Using foliage as the base, in this case the artemisia, lay two curving lines stem to stem, beginning in the horizontal center of your bookmark. Break off and discard any part of the base stem or leaves which do not carry out the desired curve.

5. Touch the end of each stem with a tiny dot of white glue and set it in position.

6. Choose two matching Victoria salvia buds for color, breaking off the stems and placing them bottom to bottom at the center of the bookmark.

7. Touch the buds with a dot of glue and attach.

8. Choose a perfect fairy rose for the center or focal point of your bookmark. Carefully break off the stem, leaving only the base of the petals showing.

9. Gently glue the fairy rose in the center, covering the stems of the artemisia and salvia, so it appears they are sprouting from the rose.

10. Choose two graceful stems of lobelia to carry out the line of the artemisia and provide a bright blue color.

11. Glue the lobelia very lightly, hiding the stem ends within the artemisia foliage.

12. Break off four or five perfect florets of Queen Anne's lace. Lay each one separately on the bookmark wherever you want a softening touch, being careful not to interrupt the line.

78

13. Place a dab of glue on the center of each floret and tuck it under the rose, one on each side. You might also want to tuck some within the artemisia, where the lobelia stem originates. The lace should appear as if it grew from the design.

14. Cut a piece of Contac paper slightly larger than the bookmark.

15. Peel back the covering and place the adhesive over the bookmark. Hold it firmly with both hands and place it straight down quickly. If you hover over the bookmark, the static of the adhesive will make your flowers reach up.

16. Smooth it with your hands.

17. Trim, following the drawn pencil lines.

18. Make a hole in one end of the bookmark with the hole punch.

19. Loop a tiny ribbon, matching the color of the rice paper, through the hole.

MAKING A FRAMED PIECE

Materials You Will Need:

Tweezers	*Professionally cut framing mat*
Matboard	*Professionally cut frame*
Ruler	*Straight edge*
Pencil	*Gum eraser*
White glue	*Foamcore (¼"-thick sheets of foam sandwiched between heavy paper, found in artist supply stores and framing shops)*

1. The matboard is the canvas on which you will make your design. With the straight edge, cut the matboard to fit into the frame you've chosen. Let's use, as an example, an 8″ × 8″ sheet of cream matboard.

2. For the design, we will create an elegant heart with red roses and green foliage. From a sheet of plain paper, cut a perfectly proportioned heart (fold in half to cut) about 4″ × 4″ at the largest point, both vertically and horizontally.

3. Make a tiny pencil dot in the perfect center of your matboard.

4. Trace lightly around the paper heart on the matboard. The heart should be in the center of the matboard with no less than 2″ as a border on all four sides. Erase the center dot when you have the pencil heart where you want it.

5. From your phone books, pull foliage with curves that match the contours of your heart. Always use foliage perfectly shaped to the pencil lines in a heart, circle or oval: you cannot force straight lines into a curve and still carry out grace of movement.

6. For a piece of this size, you will need quite a bit of foliage from which to choose. You might pick wisteria, grapevine tendrils with tiny leaves, and tiny red-tinged rose leaves, keeping in mind the same hues of green.

7. In this design, foliage provides the graceful lines; flowers add color. Choose deep red roses for drama, small red verbena flowers to carry out the color scheme, and Queen Anne's lace to soften.

8. Now you have your palette of colors: soft greens, with a deeper green accent, deep reds and cream. A rich, vibrant design will follow. The colors and textures remind me

of velvets, roses and lace. This will definitely need a rich mahogany or cherry frame.

9. Place each piece of foliage on the penciled heart line until the puzzle fits and the heart looks like it has been painted gracefully in green. Break off any parts that don't contribute to the shape, but don't be afraid to enhance it with pretty tendrils. You may need to return to the phone books for a specific curve of foliage.

10. When you have outlined the heart with foliage, begin gluing it into place, starting from the bottom of the heart and working toward the top. Remember, the heart will have tendrils and graceful lines but it should remain a perfectly proportioned heart.

The Gluing Process

Gluing is much more important in framed work because the flowers will not be held in place with Contac paper.

Glue the flowers and foliage well, but leave the pretty tapered ends free in order to tuck other flowers within. Firmly glue the stem end of the flower or foliage; it will eventually be covered. Never let any glue show. The flowers and foliage will appear as if they are naturally lying on the matboard, not glued down.

A. Pick up the flower or foliage with tweezers in right hand (if right-handed).

B. Transfer the flower to your left hand.

C. Lightly touch the ring finger of your right hand into a small amount of glue placed in a dish.

D. Ever so lightly touch the underside of the flower with glue.

E. With the little finger of your right hand, wipe the excess glue off the flower, leaving only stickiness.

F. Take the flower back with the tweezers still in your right hand.

G. Place the flower exactly where you want it in your design. Don't move it around and don't push it down hard or glue may seep out from the sides.

H. Use this method or another that works best for you throughout.

11. As you glue the foliage onto the heart, erase the pencil marks if they are not completely covered, especially if you have left a small break in the base foliage, as I often do.

11   12-13   14

12. Glue the focal rose at the bottom of the heart. Add several others for balance.

13. Add red verbena for more color. Be very careful with the red, adding color sparingly. Don't say too much. The heart should be heavier at the bottom, reaching toward a light, delicate top.

14. Add Queen Anne's lace for a softening effect and to cover any ends you do not want seen. Touch the center of the lace with a bit of glue. Be careful adding lace, or any other cluster flower such as spirea or elderblossoms, tucking it in unobtrusively; you do not want to cover up the beautiful lines of the picture. Several pieces of lace may outline the focal rose at the bottom, making it look like a valentine.

15. Turn your picture on its side and tap it gently to loosen any stray flower or foliage.

16. It is now ready for framing.

This picture could have been created with a base foliage of artemisia, using pastel colors of pink roses and blue forget-me-nots. It could be a wreath or an oval. Just remember to keep the statement simple at each step.

Two or three types of foliage give not only unity but interest and texture. Two or three complementary colors enhance the focus flower.

Framing

1. Allow enough breathing space within your picture. Don't crowd your design with the mat.

2. Remember the focus is floral art. Choose a secondary or outer mat that complements the flowers. I often use a mat the same color as the one on which the flowers are mounted.

3. Before attaching the mat, glue a strip of foamcore completely around the underside of the top, or outer, mat. This allows breathing room for the flower and also provides space for any loose petal or piece of foliage to drop and disappear, and not mar your design.

4. Attach the mat with the foamcore liner to your picture.

5. Frame, simply but professionally.

PRESERVING A WEDDING INVITATION

Materials You Will Need:

Professionally Matted Invitation   *Professionally Cut Mat*
Tweezers   *Glue*
                                         Foamcore

1. The invitation must be taken to a professional framer to be matted. The opening must be cut to perfectly fit the invitation, with only a fraction of an inch of the invitation covered. Overall, this mat and your finished piece will be $11'' \times 14''$. A second mat, of the same color, should be cut about $2''$ wide all around. This will not yet be attached.

2. Work your pressed flower design on the mat framing the invitation. You will have $2''$ at the top and $1\frac{1}{2}''$ on the sides. Borders work well, as does a simple design decorating the top right and bottom left corners. It's always fun to use flowers with special significance —lavender for devotion, and ivy for fidelity.

3. When your design is complete, glue a narrow strip of $\frac{1}{4}''$ foamcore to the underside of the $2''$ outer mat and attach to the mat on which the flowers are glued. Your gift is now ready for framing and presenting to that special couple.

$\mathcal{A}$ REGISTER OF PRESSING FLOWERS

Some flowers press better than others; shape and water content are important factors. Flowers such as tulips, irises and daffodils have a high water content. Zinnias are very thick. I have seen these flowers and others similiar in composition pressed, but I do not recommend them.

This basic list of flowers, while not exhaustive, is fairly comprehensive. I am sure, once you begin pressing, you will discover your own favorites.

TYPE OF FLOWER	COMMON NAME	COLOR	SPECIAL NOTES
Annuals	Alyssum	Pink, white, purple	Press dainty clusters.
	Annual Verbena	Navy, red	Press each flower of cluster separately, head down.
	Crystal Palace Lobelia	Deep Blue	Harvest with lovely stems and foliage attached
	Pansy	Variety	Bold color, fade quickly in pictures.
	Victoria Salvia	Blue	Harvest buds when $\frac{1}{4}$" to $\frac{3}{4}$."
Reseeding Annuals	Larkspur	Purple, blue, pink	Use some foliage and flowers. Flowers, pressed, can look like birds.
	Nigella (Love-in-a-Mist)	Blue	Use small flowers and foliage.
Biennials	Forget-Me Not	No blue like it!	Pinch tight buds off flower head before pressing. Tedious but worth the effort. Handle gently.
Bulbs	Grape Hyacinth	Blue	Harvest the smaller, sparsely flowered stems.
	Lily-of-the Valley	White	Bell-like flowers on stem, very suggestive in designs.
	Paper White Narcissus	White, yellow	Large shape, but delicate.
	Blue Pushkinia	Blue and white striped	Delicate accent.
	Scilla	Blue	Look like fairy bonnets.
	Snowdrops	Green and white	Soft bell-like flowers.

TYPE OF FLOWER	COMMON NAME	COLOR	SPECIAL NOTES
Wildflowers	Dutchman's Breeches	Cream	May float in designs like butterflies. Lovely.
	Violets	Purple	Difficult to press to retain color, but worth it. Press small foliage.
Weeds	Elderblossom	Cream	Press clusters. You may get only one head on one phone book page!
	Goldenrod	Yellow, gold	Press the young shoots.
	Grasses	Greens and naturals	Very delicate lines.
	Nightshade	Purple	Interesting shape.
	Queen Anne's Lace	White	Pick only about 25 heads and press IMMEDIATELY.
Trees	Ornamental Cherry	Pink	Lovely soft color.
	Redbud	Dark Green	Harvest the very new leaves. They're tiny hearts.
Vines	Bindweed	Green	Harvest the tendrils and vines for movement in your designs.
	Grapevine	Red, green	Harvest the tiny shoots that are used for climbing and grasping; lovely.
	Morning Glory	Green	Heart-shaped leaves and beautiful tendrils.
	Wisteria	Soft Green	Harvest tiny new leaves; poetic lines.
Shrubs	Spirea (Bridal Wreath)	White	Looks like tiny cherry blossoms. Press in clusters.
	Snowball	White, cream	Small clusters may be used as cover-ups.

TYPE OF FLOWER	COMMON NAME	COLOR	SPECIAL NOTES
House-plants	Baby Tears	Green	Dainty leaves.
	Geraniums	Red	Use buds for deep red.
	Poinsettia	Red, pink, white	Use only the tiny new leaves; striped are nice.
Herbs	Achillea Yarrow	White, pink, yellow, orange	Harvest when young and press heads facing page.
	Chamomile	White	Harvest foliage and small daisy-like flowers.
	Parsley	Green	Good green color and nice in herbals.
	Rosemary	Muted Green	Looks like little pine trees.
	Rue	Soft Green	Rounded green foliage. Pick when young.
	Sage	Gray Green	Harvest small foliage.
	Silver King Artemisia	Gray	Makes a wonderful gray base for pictures. Harvest when little buds appear but before the yellow flowers open.
	Silvermound Artemisia	Gray	Good delicate gray base for pictures. Harvest when little buds appear but before the yellow flowers open.
	Sweet Annua	Green	Two harvest times, once when plant is young and again when plant is in bud, just ready to bloom. Press quickly.
	Thyme of all types	Gray/Green	Makes wonderful base for small pictures.

TYPE OF FLOWER	COMMON NAME	COLOR	SPECIAL NOTES
Perennials	Blue Flax	Green	Harvest foliage after spring bloom. Use foliage tips.
	Columbine	Variety	Harvest when perfect. Press both buds and full flower.
	Fairy Rose (Polyantha)	Pink	Harvest leaves when tiny. Flower size is perfect. Use buds and full flower.
	Other Polyantha Roses of all colors	Variety	Harvest foliage when young for base of designs. Harvest flowers in buds and full flower. May slice buds in half vertically.
	Miniature Roses	Variety	Small leaves are beautiful. Flowers are good size for pressing.
	Hosta	Purple	Use small buds.
	Lupines	Variety	Odd-shaped flower for accent. Press each flower on stalk separately.
	Bleeding Hearts, Old Fashioned & Fern-Leafed	Pink and White	Indispensable as accent flowers, especially in heart designs.
	Virigina Bluebell	Blue	Lovely bell-shaped blue flowers. Look like fairy petticoats.
	Coral Bells	Pink	Small flowers.
	Lamb's Ears	Gray	Silver gray color, very soft. Use the small inner leaves.
	Ferns	Green	Lovely base foliage. Harvest when small.

TYPE OF FLOWER	COMMON NAME	COLOR	SPECIAL NOTES
	Astilbe	Pink, peach, white	Harvest very young shoots of flowers and foliage, end tips.
	Baby's Breath	White	Adds wispy touch to pictures. Small flowers break easily off stem after pressing.
	Violas	Blue, purple	Lovely little faces.
	Buttercups	Yellow	Press well, but may fade quickly in designs.
	Delphinium	Blue, pink	Rather cumbersome flower but good color.
	Daisy	Variety	Nice for larger pictures.

Beware: Many of these plants are poisonous. Harvest them for your designs, but don't taste them!

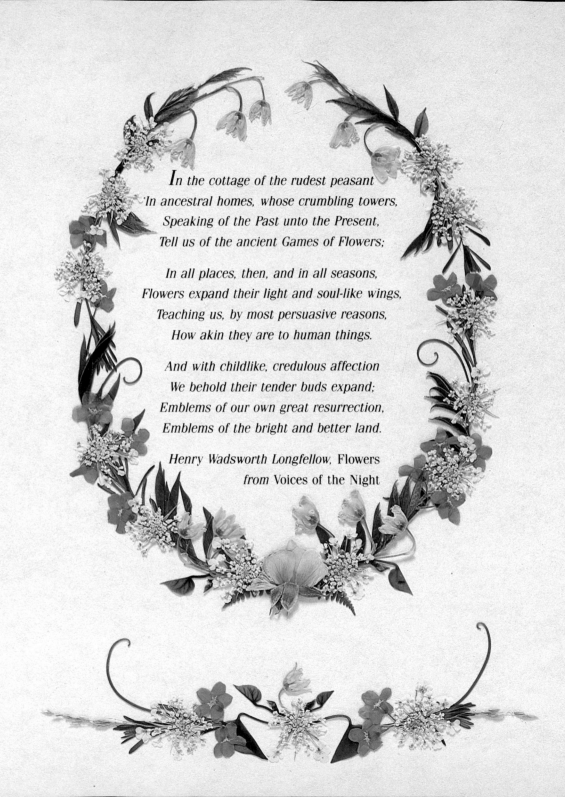

In the cottage of the rudest peasant
In ancestral homes, whose crumbling towers,
Speaking of the Past unto the Present,
Tell us of the ancient Games of Flowers;

In all places, then, and in all seasons,
Flowers expand their light and soul-like wings,
Teaching us, by most persuasive reasons,
How akin they are to human things.

And with childlike, credulous affection
We behold their tender buds expand;
Emblems of our own great resurrection,
Emblems of the bright and better land.

Henry Wadsworth Longfellow, Flowers
from Voices of the Night